Okayafrica's 2016 Year-End Book List
Literary Hub's 25 New Books by African Writers You Should Read

"*Fuchsia*, culled from robust life and a finely tuned imagination, captures mysteries of the heart and mind alongside everyday rituals. Each poem dares us line by line, and suddenly we're inside the delicate mechanism of a deep song. The magical, raw, bittersweet duende of *Fuchsia* speaks boldly. The personal history and emotional architecture of Ethiopia and Eritrea reside in every portentous poem here. But the stories, each shaped and textured by true feeling, are also ours because they beckon to us."
—Yusef Komunyakaa, author of *The Emperor of Water Clocks*

"In sometimes startlingly precise, and always musical, language, Shiferraw writes of her childhood in Ethiopia and of her contemporary life in Los Angeles with clarity, insight, and courage. Whether she is writing about butchering a sheep, uncles disappearing, a mother's mystical definition of self, of war, of poverty, of Kalashnikovs, or of hair, the words on these pages 'rummage' until they explode—into beauty."
—Gail Wronsky, author of the poetry collection *So Quick Bright Things*

"[*Fuchsia*] is deeply sensual: full of color, sense memories, and small details of life."
—Alex Dueben, *The Rumpus*

T0323963

"Color weaves through the collection, but in 'Synesthesia,' colors shoot up like flares to illuminate the trauma of fleeing home. . . . Gifted with synesthesia, the poet knows the world through color. Through her complex use of color, Shiferraw reveals home, made again through the action of memory, lending heartache, depth, and comfort to our lives."
—Mary Catherine Ford, *World Literature Today*

"These poems are always informed with a bittersweet sense of exile, of witness, and of a properly ambivalent stance toward the bewildering consumerist culture in which the writer now finds herself. Yet Shiferraw's poetry is also suffused with wonder—richly associative, Whitmanic in its linguistic energy, and totally complex, shifting without warning from wit to gravity, from self-reflection to lyric abandon. *Fuchsia* is a richly promising debut."
—David Wojahn, author of *World Tree*

YOUR BODY IS WAR

African POETRY
BOOK SERIES

Series editor: Kwame Dawes

YOUR BODY IS WAR

Mahtem Shiferraw

University of Nebraska Press / Lincoln and London

Acknowledgments for the use of copyrighted
material appear on page 72, which constitutes
an extension of the copyright page.

The African Poetry Series has been made possible
through the generosity of philanthropists Laura
and Robert F. X. Sillerman, whose contributions
have facilitated the establishment and operation
of the African Poetry Book Fund.

Library of Congress Cataloging-in-Publication Data
Names: Shiferraw, Mahtem, author.
Title: Your body is war / Mahtem Shiferraw.
Description: Lincoln: University of Nebraska
Press, [2019] | Series: African poetry book series
Identifiers: LCCN 2018038912
ISBN 9781496214133 (pbk.: alk. paper)
ISBN 9781496214508 (epub)
ISBN 9781496214515 (mobi)
ISBN 9781496214522 (pdf)
Classification: LCC PS3619.H5435 A6 2019
| DDC 811/.6—dc23 LC record available
at https://lccn.loc.gov/2018038912

Set in Garamond Premier Pro by Mikala R. Kolander.
Designed by N. Putens.

CONTENTS

Because the Body

does not break at sight

I feed it sweets, because the world
is sour in my mouth.

YOUR BODY IS WAR

Swallowing Suns

There is a picture
where you are swallowing
whole suns, small winds of fire
raging down your throat, charring everything
you have ever swallowed whole—

his mouth, their feet, chunks of poems
still bleeding with foreign blood,
these and other things
you do not know the meaning of.

It is always the same story
or different versions of the same story;

it begins with the sun
and painted palm trees
bending down without breaking
their plump leaves a song, their trunks
the size of small planets;

when you shiver, cold,
they sneeze, and suddenly

you find yourself in the land of strangers,
the land of immigrants, where people like you
forget where they came from,

because they must, because assimilation is a sin
rewarded here, because it does not carry
with itself the aroma of *shiro*, or mud or wet air,

because it is less painful to wake up every morning
and not want to paint the skies with Amharic idioms
and wave the end of hand-sewn *netela* in their direction,

because even waking up becomes an act of sorrow,
and this kind of sorrow does not let you be
who you want to be, an amalgamation of sorts,
neither alien nor human, neither foreigner
nor American or Westerner, and instead

you become a small plant, or a small tree, and your
branches grow inward, as if you are the only one
who needs to stand in the shade, as if this is
such an ordinary thing, because there are

others like you too, and even though you cannot
hear their language, and understand their voices
filled with honey and goat cheese, seeds for eyes
and abdomens filled with loaves of black bread—

even though you do not know their words,
you know their eyes, that smile they smile,
as if still hiding behind themselves,
and their backs are so broken
from worry, worry, worry, always worry
shrinking their stature, and sooner or later
you all realize

knowledge has failed you, kindness and honesty
do not actually matter, because

what is a man with an accent,
even one with blue eyes
and the fairest of skins,

what is a woman with a veiled
head, with a multitude of mouths
to feed an ocean away,

what is a boy, a girl or others
sent to follow disillusioned dreams
and instead find themselves

in constant hiding, hiding from
everything and everyone, even
from themselves, and instead they

look at you, and you look away
because you remind them
of the thing they left,
that accent they were told to hide,
that hair, that smell, that food,
that way of masking everything
behind a laughter that splits them in half.

And so you look away, as you must, as they do too
and your job is to swallow, swallow everything,
a slurpie, a pie, a chicken with eight breasts;

you swallow your light inward, so when others come
they will not notice the sadness sitting behind your eyes
and when they come, their arrogance is more sour than
old *enjera*, more bitter than loved ones lost at sea,
and you meet them with fire, having swallowed whole suns
in your life, having spent years in their shadows, because

the land of the free chooses its prodigies
like your grandmother sifts through *sirnay*,

the white ones sitting in a round tray,
the amber ones thrown to feed the chicken.

Your Body Is War (I)

because you have spent
enough time carving a wound
as big as a star, and when it's ready
you flesh it out—its colors blindfolded,
and you hold it in your hands
and you sing a forgotten song for it
until it is ripe and raw and ready to explode,
then you pick a knife, unfold your skin,
and place it right beneath it
so your blood can glow at night
and when you walk away
someone smells the scent of the firmament
emanating from your body, and they say,
this is unworldly, and it will be exactly that
because war is slow and agonizing
like how sometimes it is to love, to kill
for love, or for anything else,
and each task is so arduous, you can't let yourself
be contained, because the universe inhabits you
and your eyes are two black holes
digging through the back of your brain
appending you into white bricked walls,
and you keep telling yourself
there is no smell of war in me
but why else would this feel like madness
like a seed was planted in your stomach
and grew into a sharp spear,
and it grew out of you, and into all versions of you
and into the rest of what you thought
was you, because when it is time to stop
the body does not know it

black hole eyes cannot see
and your hands would rather busy themselves
with something new, something torn,
they touch the sand and a poem comes rushing
and it is about a black body, and a body of blackness
and you try to wash your hands, but such poems
do not go away easily, instead they stick to your skin, they
sink chiseled teeth into your bones, until all you can do
is scream, but who can hear you now, when even
your star is fallen, your eyes empty sockets of sorrow—

Madhouse

My father is a fish; he
doesn't swim, but when
he looks up, his eyes
are riverbeds, eyebrows
painted with winds,

an ever-watchful eye
splitting his forehead
and behind his back
hidden in black, black hair.

When he hears our voices
a small earthquake jolts from his eyes,
his fists clenched, because,
a father with three daughters
has many things to fear.

When he speaks,
his voice is honey
his words, poetry,
his hands tree branches,
oil skin, seeds for teeth.

Small metaphors take hold
of him, when he least expects it,
old and new Amharic
enveloping us all,
secrets we cannot understand.

Sometimes his own stories
escape quietly through the night;

he is fourteen when he carves his own soap
out of sheep fat; sixteen when he cuts
his father's hair for the last time; seventeen
when he touches the cool surface of a handgun.

There are also fleeting stories;
his beehives, his plants, the meat of
wild pigs roasted in hiding.

In sickness, we are fed
milk and honey, and when
rain falls again, we become
fish too, swimming among
the husky corn plants, our feet
drenched in mud, and we buy
karia by street shoulders—

but by then
his skin is laced in blue-gray,
constantly worried,
shoving away men with lustful eyes,
protector from lonely neighbors,
hyenas, schoolmates, and everyone else,

until it is only us
in a half-built madhouse
in the middle of nowhere.

The Art of Invisibility

I was taught
to be afraid of men
morning and day and night,

taught the art of flight
before I wrote my first words;

they will come after you
they will hunt you
they will rape you;

do not stand in their shadow, or,
do not stand at all.

Instead, learn to shrink your body
as if you were an aging fig
and to run, always run,
as fast as you can.

So I have mastered
the art of being invisible,
so breathless, if I opened my mouth
only clouds would come out,

and if you touched my flesh
it is not there, it is somewhere farther
safe behind the heads of eucalyptus
trees, behind mothers, behind women

who have eyes even in the back of
their heads, women who can hear
my woes before the sound of my
voice, women as strong as

oak trees, as tall as the city's mountains
women with a third eye, a fifth eye, an
eleventh daughter;

and I want to tell them to shut their wombs
so they can stop glancing behind their backs
or to the sides, wondering which angered demon
was sent their way, so safety cannot be a novelty,
a strange fruit hidden where they can't see it,
where only its aroma emanates slowly, slowly to the
mantels of winds, where everyone they know
everyone they once loved
will send treacherous words their way—

    what were you wearing
    what did you do
    this never happened to you

where the horror of men is nothing
compared to the ambivalence of everyone else—

and so their wombs will shut
or bleed an invisible blood, and that invisibility,
is the biggest sin—here is your veil of shame:
hide underneath it, pretend your body was not made of earth
and mud and bubbling breath, your eyes do not have light,
your mouth so foul, and your memory, so wrong! No,
it didn't happen like that.

Let us rewrite your history:

beneath the invisible veil,
you are no more.

The Suicide Chamber

Walk in silence; this is not
a place of sorrow, but one of stillness.

You are not alone—though your thoughts
are already gray, your screams soundless
and fog-thick.

These eyes, floating above your head,
this mouth attached to small things,
dismembered arms and legs
slowly crawling, making their way up, up—

this you, you do not recognize.

Instead, this is where you find
pieces of yourself, and others,
at odd hours, on quite ordinary days;

when you see your grandmother
for the first time in sixteen years, or
when remembering the unborn child, or
the dense texture of her tumor, when
longing for his breath, or when your feet
are floating above water, when something
inside of you is split in small halves, even while
staring at your reflection, or the moon's arrogant light
revealing shadows you do not want to see,

wondering what it would feel like
to fall off a bridge, and let any car swoop you by,

or jump out of the train, and let the blackness
of tunnels swallow you whole;

and drink this water, drink, drink the *tsisisat*
until it is heavy and bubbling in your lungs

thinking so fondly:

I am the daughter of the river
and to the water I shall return.

Find yourself
among the presence of others like you
ordinarily so—

somehow speaking
the same language of sorrow and shame.

This is where they come
to find relief from the world, to find
themselves, or not at all, this is where
they continue to exist in solitude,
multiples at a time, because this is easier
than anything else, easier than admitting
what they dare not say, easier
than waking up every morning, and
that is what we are reduced to,

the task of being disembodied
the small, small task of disappearing
without a sound, without a whisper of sorrow.

The Tree of My Deaths

This fire consumes me
with the appetite of a lover;

and what I want is this:

to hold it in my hands,
to kiss its flames,
to dip my hair into that
succulent orange;

all the colors I want to use
for my suicide are there—

a tender blue, the shadow of gray, the blood
of red, the purple of plum, the whiteness of the
sun, the translucence of ghosts;

I think of it like this:
I will die multichromatic.

And then there is
the blackness of it all;

the burning,
the charcoal body,
the smell of smoke.

This cannot be it, this is not
how I want it to happen;

so instead I burn
entire notebooks filled with poems,
stories I've written at night,

and the characters melt quickly, pages devoured
one after the other, and what is left is
the ash of sorrow,

and I dig a hole in the garden
by joyous *adey abeba*, and scatter ashes
and weep slowly, quietly,
as any child would.

How I tell you
years later:

there is a tree of stories in my garden
and death hangs loosely from its branches
and its leaves are a shade darker than the deepest night
and it bears no fruit, no characters, no people,
no plots; it bears no names,

the tree of my stories
the tree of my deaths.

Behind Walls and Glass

There are many places
where you can hide

but none are safe
for you to call home.

This is a land that fed you
meat and frozen vegetables,

a land that calls you
alien and immigrant,

a land that defines your self-worth
by the color of your skin,

a land where your language
is nothing but strange sounds.

This is not home;

home is a place
where you can be who you want to be

where meat comes from goat herders
where papayas are the size of cats
where God is only God
where black and brown and white
are only colors

where you fall, and a flower blossoms
in your name

where you are not asked
if you have a nickname
if you were colonized
if your ancestors were tied and sold
to the ferrous hearts of sea merchants,

if you know anyone else in the entire continent
if you were a child soldier
if you have starved.

This is not it.

This is the place to hide
behind walls and glass
behind fake accents and quick smiles
behind designer clothes
and fancy cars
and lavish trips
and dancing
and nightclubs
and short shorts
and scorned boys who want to claim your body
before you know it is yours.

This is
your hiding place:

tell no one and you'll be safe.

Your Body Is War (II)

When men tell you this
you do not know who you are;

men with long arms and lurid eyes
bleeding an old blood, speaking
a thing you have heard before.

They say, your body belongs
to them, or the war,
something you will yourself to forget,

though you feel parts of you missing
eaten away slowly in broad daylight.

What they leave: not one
wound, but these:

the flowers of one thousand
wounds, within thousands more, so
small and so deep, resting comfortably
within your walls.

There is nothing
left to do.

You are sick, but
this sickness does not let you grieve,
or be, or believe.

If they ask, you have been at war before,
or, you were it, and you have spent
so many years in wandering, having
forgotten the bone sound of sleep, or

the smell of things unbleeding.

Instead, when men come,
you hide, and they
find you anyway.

You think you are invisible
and you must be
because that rustling sound
must not be there, those hands
must not be reaching under your shirt
and that voice belongs
only to the devil.

When you are alone
the whispering becomes water,
murmuring things
you do not want to hear
because that would have you
stand so tall, so unremarkable,
naked flesh and bare bones
breaking open once more.

But this, this you, you know;
the danger of being so utterly vulnerable,
being present, or worse, being noticed,
spotted among the thinning crowd
when you are hiding, not recognizing
your face in the mirror, because
the one who looks back

has a blinded eye
and ears slashed, and a
permanent smile etched
from earlobe to earlobe.

This, you should do:
feign a great sleep
upon their arrival,
a small death.

What is it to you anyway—

you thought you were dead
but the dead have no more fear
and you have water-waves of it,

so many you escape at night
to fill the oceans, and the oceans
spit a black spit back to you
and when you come back
there is nothing left.

You
are not there,
but your body is:

war—

ash, ash, ash,
now dead, now a ghost,
walking among the tombstones of men
calling their names one by one

thinking them ravagers—a smell
you have taught yourself so well, and with
each scar you draw a new wound, hundreds more
showing up to drink sunlight, thick shards of glass
underneath your skin, cutting your flesh, the names
of men etched beneath each bone

containing this—

no ordinary war
no ordinary body

into a thoughtless spree, selves multiplied
as many as the wounds,

black ocean
black master
black festering heart.

Ash and Blue

The inevitability
in certain things:

the sky holding
thoughts, and folding

them back slowly.

Oak wood aging
with time, its lines the

center of the earth, rings
resurfacing upon each other.

Moss thickening, the
smell of morning air and

carrying it through the day.

The delicate composure
of small objects—

a pen, an unloved desk,
papier-mâché ghosts.

One moment, the
self, the next, ash.

Body of Punishments

You crave the unknown
like your body craves punishment;

a father throwing
the sleeping body of his daughter
down the stairs,

the hands of a homeless man struck down
with a bullet,

the corpses of chairs and tables
thrown against walls,

a belt's peeled skin
because of too many lashings,

the body left untouched
after so much fumbling.

It is easier
to distance yourself
from it all, anything that can numb
this grayness out of you.

Remember what this body
wants to crave:

sunbathing in the Spring,
a soft kiss on the throat,
tickling hair in the back of the neck,
ocean water under the feet,
rain all over its skin.

This body of punishments
wants to be remembered
for what it could have been:

a home for the displaced.

Like a Lover's Quarrel

It begins on a moonless night
like any other;

I am sitting on the top bunk
waiting for starlights to exhale
their ghostly presence.

That is where I am, mostly,
among the presence of ghosts
and though I am only twelve

I am convinced I am one too
because how else can I explain

this removal, this detachment,
a disassembling of selves,

heads rested on blue walls,
razor sharp nails sinking into white pillow;

how to explain this conflict

continuous, intimate
like a lover's quarrel
showing up in the middle of the night
in the middle of a night terror
in the middle of a thought—

Water

It is autumn
when I first see it:

the light of knitted rain,
the smell of wet mud
water in the shoes.

Is this water the same
as any water; as the water
that wants to kill me—

The Curse of Ishmael

I call you Ishmael
son of Abraham, curse
of my curse,

son of a handmaid
servant to the devil.

I call you assailant
an eye on your forehead
the forehead a map
to the bodies you wear
slowly, slowly.

I call you brother, friend;
the languages I speak
refusing to contain this you,
this version of me.

The fear in your eyes
as your father
takes you to slaughter,

the fear in my eyes
as I am replaced
over and over again.

Something about our fathers
not knowing our worth
connects us.

Something about our mothers too
grief-stricken, made to obey
the men they love,

remade in the images
of God.

Call me water; when you
are wandering through desert dunes
with your mother, I appear
as if commanded by God.

You drink me
and never know
I saved you.

This is
our curse too.

Black and Blue

The first time we see the ocean
it is coated in black
and blue.

I see: black,
she sees: blue.

We can hear it through the night,
a slight rumbling, crashing of waves
into white sands.

Every now and then
we go back to collect pebbles
from its feet, polish their
smooth surface, kiss their
forehead, and store them in a clear jar.

It is a sign:

sometimes they will find their way
back to us, replacing our eyes
so everything we see
is drenched in water;

the black and blue
calling us with the same name

and when we are completely submerged
this thing we have become
leaves us be.

Death by Trains

I am in Italy
in the arms of a boy
when I contemplate suicide by trains again;

it is not the first time
I find myself attracted
to their speed, their light, their lightning bolt.

I ask the same question:

what if I jump?

He says, *not now,*
but he means, *not here.*

I want to say,
I need accomplices
to hold *her* down;

she is unafraid

of things moving, things stagnant, things poised,
things sharp, things enveloping, things tall,
things suffocating, things undead, things numb.

I am afraid
of everything.

Mostly of the way I keep thinking
about skulls, and the merciful beheading
of chickens, and the lost songs of goat herders,

and of myself.

Whoever I am,
whoever we are.

The Memory of the Body

How it reacts
to a world of drowning

how sutures and ligaments
are marred within, and if you

touch one, they all swell
ready to explode.

How to distance this ocean
blue or white, coating the earth
head to toe to womb,

how to think of this
and not see death all around.

How to forget
things done to this body
in soliloquy, or how to undo
so much forgetting.

How to unlearn invisibility,
how not to move obediently
deep into the night under
muffled breaths,

how to tie thousands of knots
upon knots, how to hold small roars
within, right beneath a coarse throat,
how to later swallow whole strawberries
still bleeding of juice and water;

how to shrink
without disappearing,

how to unearth the truth,
and if so, how to let it fester
slowly, slowly,
into the histories
of our leaving.

Your Body Is War (III)

Here is what you know:

as a child, you were sent to war
and though you didn't know it then,
or now, it stayed with you long after
claiming parts of your body you knew
not to exist, thinking that could
heal you from old afflictions, arising new.

You were always free to taste the apple
but never to see your nakedness, or his,
so luminous, calling your name
into the dark abyss.

The taste of it
you'll never forget.

What was then, what is now:

your body, already shaped into
a long spear, skin spiking little thorns,
tongue and eyes on fire, and sorrow,
a long-quilted metal armor.

Your breath: beneath, an
invisible shield.

This thing you are sent to kill
has no name, no recognizable scent,
and sometimes bears your face

on a white shadow, startling you
when you least expect it.

There is nothing here;

not shame, not lust, nor
wandering eyes. But what is:

a body torn, childlike or not,
organs clenched from an old horror,
and a seeping sensation swerving through
and through.

Open.

Once, this body
housed an intricate war—

does it matter if you were the foot soldier,
the general, or the horse running into battle,
does it matter if you were held prisoner for years
and found yourself as the guard, and sometimes,
even the glim eyes of a gray death.

Open this body:

purples and poison-berries
have taken shelter here
and a continuous bleeding
like a new river born
on the throat of a green lake
where you were once born,
twice in death, endlessly longing.

Genesis

And darkness was upon the face
but the face was not yours.

What was: the waters
or the firmament
illuminated with His words.

And so it was:
waters gathered under
one place, whether you or
dry land

this earth so good
it bears the fruits of many names
yielding seeds of every kind,
and among them, you.

And once, you were a word
or a thought, and with the Beginning.

All things in you, all under
your dominion.

And in you, a life you cannot own,
nor neglect, and in the world
a darkness you can comprehend.

This darkness, a witness
to your kind, the beginning
to your end.

And this light, a likeness
you cannot unhinge from.

Because before
you were acquainted with death
you knew the face of life
and light; and it was good to you.

This face, the fruit of darkness
and light, all at once

a new seed
a new kind.

The Old Tree

Sometimes you think of this
as fabric, because you see the skin
fold and unfold, dry and burn,
the softness emaciated as if it was nothing.

Other times you think this is
what it is: only a body
housing something new, something strange
something like you,

but then you would have to think
of yourself as a stranger
and strangers have not been good to your body.

At times, it also becomes a vessel of sorts
carrying sorrow-quenched eyes, a mouth of fire,
and a spirit so gray, it almost looks black;

but then you would have to consider
how black once saved you
how black came back for you
how you were told *you are black*
and found it odd, and familiar,
because that part of you, you already knew.

Sometimes you are also told
it houses the divine, though you cannot fathom
how, or even why, why would the divine choose
to have its resting place here, here where mad things
happen in broad daylight, where everyone's eyes watch eagerly
and say nothing of the blackness, to you or anyone else,

where they say nothing of the madness that will follow you
day after day, especially at night, when mourning for a loss,
this loss, has become so customary you almost miss it.

But most times you think of this
as a tree: a eucalyptus tree, an oak tree,
a willow tree, and you can clearly see
these branches, so long they can reach
the back of your head, and hold it in place,
and when you move, your leaves

fall, as part of you will always do,
and new ones grow back again,
sturdier, greener, lovelier, and
birds rest on your branches
and sing songs in beautiful languages
you didn't know existed,

where the lonely and the hunters
seek for your shade, where ordinary people
whisper their secrets, where your roots
are so deeply entrenched with the earth
they explode upon concrete roads, and push
upward, always upward,

until you see the naked horizon
and you can already smell the ocean breeze
and there, yes, there you can think of this
as what it could be: the world contained
in flesh, and sorrow, and bones, and ash,
the world contained in you, and you
spread all over the world
like the branches of an old tree.

The Wrong Kind of Dream

She dreams of long hair, this
little black girl, slicked, soft
on the skin and gentle on the scalp.

Whether she sees it
attached to white bodies
or finds it herself in a dreamless
sleep, is another thing.

But this kind of hair
she can tie into a knot,
wrap into one fishtail,
already seeing the translucence
emanating from her face.

This kind of dream
she can achieve quickly;

though what sits
so stubbornly on her head
refuses to flow with the winds
and instead claims her entirely.

Brush it to the side
and it hurts,

downward
and it hurts,

and up, up
hurts even more.

In days like these
a quiet scream unleashes itself
deep from her gut, though
she knows not to be too vocal
about her personal complaints.

This dream of otherness
consumes her slowly
or quickly, depending
on the tide of her strength,

whispering things she does not
let herself forget

white women in TV commercials
flaunting blonde, luscious hair,
saying,

> *this is not what you should look like*
> *your type is not the right type*
> *your hair is not the right hair*
> *if not bleached, cut, shaved*
> *or straightened—*

until she sits disembodied
and one day finds parts of herself
walking down the street

her floating head
impaled on a mannequin's white body

her paler and long-lashed eyes
on the face of a little girl

and this dream
paints everything she sees,
everything she is;

who has the right to tell her
she's dreaming the wrong dream.

Your Body Is War (IV)

Small riots take place
underneath your skin.

You want to collect small pebbles
and push them against your orbits

because when you open your eyes
there is only black ocean and white sand.

This is where it all happened—
an evening like any other,
a day like any other,
a monster like any other
sitting right beside you
rain falling in slow bouquets
the salty taste of warm tears
painting your upper lip blue.

Lift one hand to the air;
do you see where the tip bleeds?

That is where you must plant a seed
and snatch it before it grows away.

But war is war before it even begins,
before you wallow your eyes in grief
before you arm yourself,
before everything else.

You want to see this differently;
—and who wouldn't—

but the voices are too many
and they say you are unarmed
and they call you small
and they thrust small razor blades
down your throat, and send
scarred men your way, and you are
only a body, only a bleeding heart,
invisibility your greatest shield, faith
your armor, but when you look up

you are not here: only a body,
pebbles for eyes, branches for limbs,
algae in your abdomen, bones white as sand,
your ligaments only poems
emerging beyond the page, and you are:

a ghost, and ghosts do not hear poems,
ghosts do not cry, ghosts do not live,
ghosts with a headless body, skin full
of scars, cells from a bleeding sea,

the ancient markings of a body at war
constantly at war, constantly in terror,
a body strained, a body wronged, a body
disappearing, a body wrought.

Journey with Dante

In the earliest of days
I stand with Dante; he wants to
take me to the forest, but I am *la lupa*,
and he does not know.

When I open my jaws
a river flows away slowly
translucent clouds on battered ground
and somewhere a monk is howling
and I become a boat, rocking
I Promessi Sposi to land, and the
pen that writes us does not see me.

Dante wants to know
what's a little black girl doing
learning the first syllables of Latin,

and I want to say, *Ms. Angelou*,
but I have not found eloquence
in words yet.

We climb a tall mountain
and there, spread like wildflowers,
are the letters of *Abelardo & Eloisa*
and I want to kiss their handwriting—

but alas young Werther awaits, and he
is impatient and *folle*, and wants to know

what am I doing there
following the trail of long-bearded men
into solitude.

But I am too diligent
to think of such things;
besides, Shakespeare in Italian
is Shakespeare in love

and I know a little about love
though I am only fifteen, I know because
Petrarca has engraved his sonnets in my heart
and I am convinced they were written for me
though I am neither fair-skinned nor gray-eyed
though I am not like the youngsters in Decameron
though I am only in love with small, small poems
I can unpack quickly
and hide beneath my tongue

but I let them all come in
one after the other
their words like mighty swords,

Saba in his Vanitá,
Calvino & his mistress moon
and I let them all in
especially Leopardi,

I let him build small sculptures all over my arms
and in my torso, and my legs, and he wants to take me
with him, in this *naufragar*, yes, my *naufragar*,
but he is too late.

Pavese has already embalmed my body
and earth and mud is all that is left
and earth and mud we eat, earth and mud
until Levi descends, and then, what are we?

We are not human.

They already know
how I write poems in small booklets
and math worksheets,

they know how I will give
my poems to anyone
even to G., who will be enchanted by those words
so enchanted she thinks of them as her own,
so enchanted she sends them to editors
and when I see this poem, published with her name,
it is not mine
because my poems are not mine
my words not mine,

and they already know
how it starts then,
how I am never where I am supposed to be
how I will burn my stories
in the backyard, when Father is away for the day,
how I refuse to write poems
but they still bleed out of me
and how I am always running
running and running

and there to catch me,
Montale, Quasimodo, Pascoli, Libertá—

and when I look up
the sun is setting again
and everything is quiet again
but a thousand soldiers' feet
erupting the earth into a crude awakening
their ships already sailed, already armed;

is that Virgilio? Could I be present
among these men, could I be
on the island of Ulysses, eternally
waiting for his return, could it
be me on the shoulders of Enea
on his way to Rome?

Dante smiles; we are in the land of poets, in
the land of language

but when I open my mouth
when my pen spits
words come out half broken, pencil sharp

and they are in Italian
though I think of them as colors
though I think of them in Amharic
though I shape them with dreams

they still come out in Italian
glazed in chocolate and music

glazed in this language that
kept my people prisoners and
renamed the cities of Eritrea
in this language of love and fascism
this language that built barricades
between the black African and white European
this language that cleaned itself squeaky
from my people's history, my people's culture,
this language that calls us

barbari, ignoranti, negri, immigranti

this same language
that rocks us to sleep
and forces down our throats
the history of its people
the history of the only people who matter
the Greeks, the Romans, the Westerners,

this language that shaves off
centuries of our kingdoms and our kings
this language that takes credit
for our cities' architecture, our roads
that sheepishly thrusts itself
into our own language,

macchina, forchetta, ospedale

this language that sleeps with our women
and breeds brown babies, and outcasts them quickly

meticci, mulatti

this language of poetry
this language of sorrow

and I want to tell Dante,
I was scorned for not knowing
how to speak my language

Amharic, Tigrinya,

because I was the girl
with neck bent, eyes squinted,
learning the language of a foreign land
the language of General Graziani

the language of Mussolini
learning to assimilate quickly
learning to smile and not dissent
even as I hear teachers say

she cannot be this good
she is not Italian

but what they mean is

she is not white

and even though Dante is so proud
a B is an F for a diligent student
and I carry it with me everywhere
when I hear strangers say

pasticceria, pizza, amore mio

when we visit Gondar, and Bahr Dar
and we visit the sights of massacres
and through Arba Minch
seeing the caves of monks burned alive
bare skulls adorning the sprawling feet of trees

I carry it with me to Asmara
when I hear my grandmother say
how they used to drink from different faucets
and kicked away from the white man's bathroom
and how they were forbidden
from the streets of their own city

because that language is too white,
too clean to wipe itself off
from our dirty, black skin;

but when I turn around
we have reached a place
I do not know—

At the Mad Man's

A madman guards our door;

others think we are here
because of what we have been told,

because we are not capable
of loving ourselves.

We say,

how American of you
to think of such things;

we are here
in the ring of ice and gray

because we are in fact in love
with the idea of the world
without our presence.

When we hear others
talk about us in the singular way
we want to warn them;

we are many
and we come as quick as the wind
and stay stronger than mountains
and our thoughts are multiplied
and diced a thousand different ways
and one brain, one body is not enough
to contain all of it, and our skin bursts

with thought bubbles
and so we let sharp razors cut our wrists
and wait for blood to gurgle out slowly,

a small exhale
in a breathless world.

Water Dreams

This must be
where I come to die;

where the nectar of barbed cacti
and honey-glazed breads wander endlessly,
among the silver of city sidewalks
suddenly opening up into deep burrows.

In this, my dreams have colors
the brilliant shades of molten metal—

in this, someone calls my name
but when I answer, only the sharp edges
of a skeleton show up.

This, where I fall in flight too—

the burning water or blue, the hope
of drowning too quickly, spear-eared
dogs jumping off to bite the arches of my feet.

This waking is filled with screaming, though
silence succumbs us all: in this, I become we,

and when a hazy sleep catches us again
our bodies are already engulfed in gray flames
and the sound of something tearing apart
into thousands of pieces we cannot recollect
becomes a distant memory of the night.

The Body Book

I found a book
and it was a body

and it was a book
and it was a bird.

I found a body
and it was a woman
and it was a man

and it was silent.

I found a woman
and she was a man
and he was a book

and they a body.

I found a silence
and it was the body
and it was the bodies

and it was new.

Conversations with Self

THE EMPTY ROOM

Begin in the middle of a thought;
between a longing so old

deeply lodged into your backbones
you don't feel it any longer.

Small pieces of blood and gold
make up your heart,

which is to say

small pieces of you
scattered everywhere.

Go to dinner, go to drinks,
go and laugh with friends
or strangers, or yourself.

You are a stranger too
in a strange, small world
filled with tall trees
bearing your name on their branches,
trees blooming at night
white and purple flowers
with smoldering petals, where
you had once etched your stories.

This, or another story,
it does not matter.

You think you know,
but you don't.

Who does?
Who knows you, knows
this, this thing hidden
beneath your skin?

See how it glows at night
when everyone else is asleep
in a dreamless world, see how
it seems to breathe a different air,
and exhale only poison, like the
greenest plant in an empty room.

There's the metaphor
you've been looking for:
you are the empty room.

And now sit:
your poison is just settling in.

Conversations with Self

DYING IN BEAUTY

after Gail Wronsky

Sometimes at night
you find yourself screaming
a quiet scream.

It does not scare you,
but the sorrow you feel afterward
will tear you apart.

I do not know
how to do this;

how to be sad
without hopelessness

how to hope
without despair;

it's not a decision
but an advanced sense of being,

staying in such brilliant silence.

Perhaps you were unloved
or loved too much, a love
so perverse, it kept you hidden
in one room, white walls and

cold glass underneath, water
only to prolong your aching,
though still in beauty.

Dying in such beauty:

that is something
you'll never know.

Conversations with Self

BLUE-BLACKS

Things that are not new:
dying your hair blue, or,
blue-black;

thinking of your hair
as yours,

yourself
as yours;

knowing different shades of blue
as you have known belonging
with things you cannot claim
as your own—

something about these blues
living within, carving you
from the inside out.

These days, someone else
inhabits this body, perhaps
someone you do not want to be.

The soliloquy of these thoughts
all amassing to one, is bluest too:

you are not you.

What you know to be true:
the hunger, the sadness,
the white madness.

This kind of beauty
is all vain.

Staying with you: only
the blue-blacks, then
and now, and through
multiple selves.

Conversations with Self

NAKEDNESS

When you are not looking
something within you dies;

when you do not hear
it is torn apart.

Look, these broken pieces
are too shattered to mend
so why bother—

what is at stake here anyway.

What it takes: honey, mostly,
a sweetness so strong
it turns everything from blue to gold,
from gold to sickly green,

because at least being sick
means you're still alive
and two alive
is better than one dead—

Or one longed for in absentia.

The luxury of thinking
you are in *this* alone;

have you not seen others
with the same nakedness
as yours,

have you not heard their wailing
deep into the night
and found yourself wondering
how it can be so dreadful
and beautiful at the same time—

This is how it happens anyway;
when you are not looking,
on such an ordinary night.

This, is what you have done.

Conversations with Self

THE RIVER

When it calls you
do not dare
welcome yourself
in its spaces.

You are ugly.
You are invisible.
You are fat.

How dare you think
you descend from this river.

Train this body
to occupy small, small spaces,
train your eyes to close shut
and unsee his.

This invisibility
is becoming,

it is what turns you
into water again, sitting
beneath the smoky falls,

the bleeding pouring
with river matter,

singing the song of the bluebird,
wafting through new and old scents—
sugary, green—finding yourself

among cluttered algae, and your sleep
inhabits mud-waters, and you swim
with glossy animals, and bathe
naked under the sun, and you turn
so white, so blue, so green,

you are almost beautiful.

The Yellow Woman

Your blood is yellow,
like daisies sprouting in *Meskerem*
in your flower city, yellow as in

the light that fogs
dangerous things hanging
behind the restless shadows
of teenage boys,

yellow as in absence, then screams
of mothers gathered neatly
between acacias and
speeding taxi vans, yellow as in

the crown of the lion on a city bus,
while visiting your brother in jail,
or was it school, or the airport?

You can't remember because
yellow is everywhere.

Everywhere you look,
everywhere you are, a sense
of loss follows you slowly, slowly,

dragging itself across
the streets and through
mountains, and it carries with it
a smell, like fire, like earth after rain,
like roasted corn heads and burned coffee,

it smells of *berbere* and *mitmita*,
of sour *enjera* and hot milk

and incense, a faint scent of honey-dust
and leaves in the sea,

and it is a scent
that attaches itself to your body,
to each limb separately,

to your ugly face, your grass hair,
even underneath each organ,
and into your blood vessels,

as if it is the only thing
you need to sustain you,
to carry you through each day,
unnoticed and unsought,

as if it is your only life source,
your supply to breathe
the heavy air of foreign countries,

and if they cut your skin open
you are convinced
yellow blood will spill out quickly,

and though they think
you are black, or brown,

you want to tell them

I am yellow,
I have yellow in me

and it does not
let me die.

The Fruit Mother

My mother is a cactus fruit, but her thorns
have been plucked out carefully, and when
they cut her open, she bleeds a sweet blood
and squirts out quickly from her coat.

She is also a mango. She hides underneath
beds of papaya, because mango eaters will come
after her, because they will want to put her in
a plastic bag with others like her, and choke
her quickly, before she has the chance to bruise.

My mother is also *accat*. She can only be found
in the arid weathers of East African depressions.
She looks like she has been traveling for centuries
and only found rest in the hands of sea merchants.
When they eat her, hands grab her whole body,
nudge it until she is undone, throw her head in
dusty rocks and sink their teeth wistfully.

She is also *gaba*. Small being hiding underneath
others, trying to go unnoticed, undisturbed. When
she is sold, it is usually to children, and she will sit
uneaten for days, warm in their pockets, and she will
sing to them until they are fast asleep and roll out of
their nest quickly, falling to the ground, finding her
way out of closed white walls.

She is also a small banana, or a batch of small bananas
and if one wanted to pick her, she would have to climb
the tallest tree in Gurage, where she has gone for a yearly
pilgrimage, and slowly suck the sweetness out of her, and her

skin would be laid on the floor and beaten to make bread and
butter. She would feed only the good-spirited ones.

Here, my mother is a berry. We do not know what kind.
Sometimes she is a strawberry, bright and bold and bitter
bloodying our teeth. Other times she comes as a blackberry,
her hair wrapped in small moons, her eyes unlit, and when
she speaks, it is soft, it is a song, it is a mourning
that does not let you weep. At times, she is also blueberry,
ashen and small, collecting herself in small
batches in the way only she can, then spread out yet again.

But in her truest self, she transforms into *beles* again, and
she is armed with horns, back in the white city, and her father
is not gone, instead he smiles and pats her in the back,
and scares away those who have come for her, and
gently wraps her body with its thorns in a clear bowl
and puts her away. That is where she'll stay until
we come to wake her.

Ghost Procession

All the ghosts of life
assemble before us;

some are ghosts
we didn't know we had,
some from our past, some
the thin shadows of their ghosts.

It is not a particular place
nor is it a country, a city, a house.

They are dressed in black;
a veil of feathers and lost breaths,

and when they speak
their voices are one, and many
at the same time,

and when they speak
our mouths fall off
because these are our words,
our chants, our prayers

because even silence
is taken away from us

reshaped and repurposed
until it is not ours anymore.

Your Body Is War (V)

A resting place
for the dead, earth full
of worms and white bones.

You do not look like
your mother, because your
bricks are snow, and not
like your father, because
your hair is fire, and not
like your brother because
water is not within you.

Your body is small,
and invisible, and when you
wake up at night

it is covered in poems—
stained ink adorning your skin
capturing moments you do not recall.

Sometimes you hide it
underneath a shadow

because you cannot undo the past,
because you cannot unsee yourself.

Your body needs you,

not like it would need a missing limb
or a blinded eye, or a sewn mouth,
not like it would need another body,
another self, another story;

but like it needs your unveiling,
it needs you to kill the stench of shame
the fears, the dreams of horror,

like a child needs its mother
like a child needs anything
like a child,

it needs you
to wake up.

ACKNOWLEDGMENTS

This book has been seen by many, through light, through strength, and endurance. Through poetry, through war. This book owes so much of its thinking to the strong and fearless women I am surrounded by; my mother, survivor of many wars; my aunts, swirling lights among dark men; my beautiful, beautiful girlfriends, with whom I bear the burden of our collective bodies, our collective histories. Thank you to these brilliant women—mothers, sisters, friends, lights that shine my way through the darkest days, who trust me with their stories. Thank you to my siblings, my armors against the world. Thank you to my husband, my everything. Thank you to the African Poetry Book Fund, for all the work you do, visible and invisible, to bring new voices from the continent. A special thank you to Chris Abani, Kwame Dawes, Matthew Shenoda, Aracelis Girmay and the editorial board, for their tireless support, and their faith in my work. Thank you to God, for giving me this language; this new clarity, a better seeing. Thank you to *Mamma*, for allowing me the freedom to read and write, when you couldn't; with every poem, I carry your wounds on my body.

To my daughter, I write this book, because you inhabited a body filled with wars, and made it your home; because you gave it hope and filled it with new lights.

Previous versions of the following poems have been published in the chapbook *Behind Walls & Glass* (Georgetown KY: Finishing Line Press, 2015): "The Tree of My Deaths"; "Behind Walls and Glass"; "Ash and Blue"; "Body of Punishments"; "Like a Lover's Quarrel"; "Water"; "Black and Blue"; "Death by Trains."

"Your Body is War (I)" and "The Old Tree" appear at *Hermeneutics Chaos* (2017).

Earlier versions of "Your Body Is War (IV)," "The Art of Invisibility," and "Swallowing Suns" were published by *Prairie Schooner* (Winter 2017).

The poem "Behind Walls & Glass" has been included in *Coiled Serpent: Poets Arising from the Cultural Quakes and Shifts of Los Angeles* (Los Angeles: Tia Chucha Press, 2016).

Earlier versions of "The Yellow Woman" and "Mad House" appear in *Voices from Leimert Park Anthology, Redux* (Hollywood CA: Harriet Tubman Press/ Tsehai Publishers 2017).

"Journey with Dante" was published by *At Length* (2017).

IN THE AFRICAN POETRY BOOK SERIES

Seven New Generation African Poets: A Chapbook Box Set
Edited by Kwame Dawes and Chris Abani
(Slapering Hol)

Eight New-Generation African Poets: A Chapbook Box Set
Edited by Kwame Dawes and Chris Abani
(Akashic Books)

New-Generation African Poets: A Chapbook Box Set (Tatu)
Edited by Kwame Dawes and Chris Abani
(Akashic Books)

New-Generation African Poets: A Chapbook Box Set (Nne)
Edited by Kwame Dawes and Chris Abani
(Akashic Books)

New-Generation African Poets: A Chapbook Box Set (Tano)
Edited by Kwame Dawes and Chris Abani
(Akashic Books)

To order or obtain more information on these or other University of Nebraska Press titles, visit nebraskapress.unl.edu. For more information about the African Poetry Book Series, visit africanpoetrybf.unl.edu.